HEAR MEN!

RAUDRA SERIES, OCT '22

JYOTI PRAKASH

To my brotherhood!

Contents

PREFACE

This small work of mine is a little attempt to address what I feel for gender. I must have been biased at times. That will be my fault in craftsmanship, but again I must admit the fact that all cannot be pleased with equal consistency.

I also aim not to please anyone. I have written this work only keeping in mind a limited proportion for what is happening in reality. Reality is ever expanding; everyday something new happens. I may have used some outdated ideas, but they can never be rejected.

Any homo sapien is at a junction of mental, emotional, physical and psychological alleys. I have not touched upon certain parts too.

At any given point of time, all the possible ideas cannot be squeezed into pieces of paper. I therefore reserve all other possibilites for some other future works.

Jyoti Prakash
September 2022
Balasore

Acknowledgements

This work is dedicated to all men I have ever known. Growing up in an enviroment where men work like anything to sustain the family and women working really hard to ensure the family is running, I could not keep myself away from writing this work.

I personally feel men and women are physically different, they are built different and made different. A potter makes both pot and a bowl of mud. Coincidentally, both the untensils can store water in then. But the way water is taken out of them or poured into them, is essentially different.

Sometimes I feel sad for my father, for I could never be as hardworking as him. From him I learnt there are three matters:

First matter, or the things of home. These issues, incidents and events should never be discussed outside the doors of home.

Second matter, or the things of outside. These issues, incidents and events should never cross the doors of home and come in. They are meant to stay outside.

Third matter, or the zone of portmanteau. Certain issues shall come inbetween the two mentioned matters.

But where does the issue of 'gender' fall among these groups?

I must not forget my brothers from Central University of Odisha, Koraput, with whom I had spent some great time. I categorically thank Sourav Chandra, Dhaniraj Nag and Raju for being my constants there.

Prologue

The boy or men or male, irrespective of what I call them or you all call them, he shall stay the same. He is anonymous. He looks at the world both in a naive and critical manner.

He is at fault and so are the other girls or ladies or females. No one is perfect.

This imperfection is harmonic.

I

An Interview

He desired only if he could move on like the moving bus, he was sitting in. On the last seat of the old bus, on an old, rugged dust-soaked maroon seat, he sat still. Mourning for his loss, he was silent. The day never did pass the way he thought it to be.

The tie that made him confident was now strangling him and pushing him to some unseen deathyard.

The blazer that made him feel cozy was making him breathless now.

The wristwatch that made him look gentleman now was just a silent symbol of shame.

The file that he had held with great pride was now heavier than any metal he had known.

Wiping his tears through the corner of his foggy glasses, he has only one question. "Why not me?" Why not him, was tearing him from within. He was torn amidst his tears and fears.

"What shall happen now?" he questioned him.

A part of him answered, "what else? Things will go on as they used to go on!"

It had been a bad day for him. He was all ready for the day. It was his day; he had his day but could make it. His day however was far from him.

Early in the morning, after taking the blessings, tucking the shirt in his pants, and combing his hair, he left for his interview. It will be painful to say what interview it was. I wish to keep it in me.

"May I come in Madam?" he asked after opening the door a little.

His one-hour long journey in the bus had made him look dizzy. His perfect look was gone. To relieve himself from the heat, he has slackened his tie, he was ready to open his shirt too. But his white shirt had already got spots of dust and stain from the pitted seat.

"Your bio-data please!"

He opened his files and handed his resume that he had created cautiously and had carried with an even greater caution.

"Good morning, Madam, I am…" he formally introduced himself.

Looking at his sweaty condition, one of the five fellows sitting on the other side of the table asked, "Mr..... Do you need some time to make yourself comfortable?"

With a broad daylight smile, he said, "I am comfortable sir."

"Is the room too cold?"

Keeping his head straight, "no sir, its perfect!"

"Did you have your breakfast?" someone else asked.

"Yes sir, I did have my breakfast. I generally do not skip it?"

Just as he finished, the mouth on the left asked, "on what occasions do you generally skip your meals?", stressing hard on 'generally'.

He again smiled, "on days when I am busy and run out of time."

"What makes you busy?"

Making no serious expressions and brining no emotions in his tone he started, "with all due respect ma'am, I have seen my father working hard in the fields. The certificates and courses that I now hold and say with pride and say with pride that I have earned them; it will be a matter of grave shame if I do not recognize the sacrifices that they have made."

He took a pause and continued, "it wasn't just my efforts that have made me reach here. The blazer, tie, and shirt that I have put on me, to put on a great show of modernism; I feel they are the true moderns or perhaps ultra-moderns. I sometimes go to help him in his work."

His tone started shaking. "There are days when my old father with skin sticking to his bones, age consuming his muscles, leaves for the fields before sunrise. I cannot help with that, and I too follow him." He stopped.

"Is that what makes you different from others – helping you father in farming?"

He looked at the questioner and smiled again. "Sir, no one is born different. Everyone's born the same way you and I were born. But the way one is taken care of varies. The way I grew up in my family is what makes me different!"

"Can you elaborate it?"

He began, "I was given no such stress when I was a child. But getting no stress is also stress. In my village I saw my friends going to fields when they were of the age ten or eleven. But I was not allowed to go until I was 15! I was permitted only after I passed tenth board!"

"What was your score?"

"As I have mentioned in my resume, I had scored 91 percentage in my boards. I was the district topper!"

The third face from the left adjusted his spectacles and scanned though the printed paper. "Being the only son of my parents, I always wanted to be a resource to my parents! But my father was wise enough who knew the strength of education," he added.

Perhaps it was the fourth mouth that asked, "so what do you aspire to become once you are here with us?"

"I will try to look up and more. Limitations are everywhere, so are solutions. I want to become that fly which can escape all the slaps, before being beaten to death."

"But a fly is meant to burn isnt it?"

"Yes sir, it must burn and turn into ashes. Fire and life have rivalry, but life is incomplete without fire. Any live wire can take life, but it lights a bulb that prevents any accident in the dark."

The fifth head asked, "aren't you being too much optimistic?"

"There can be never too much optimisms! Too much pessimism is poisonous. It's better to die with a smile rather than suffering to some poison."

"Don't you think death is something that we must avoid?" it was the central head.

"Arrival is always attached to departure. If there is arrival, there must be a departure. We cannot be too much selective. Therefore, human as species is suffering. We want comfort and we want only good. But nature isnt built like that. There shall always be a gap. This chasm of evil and good runs simultaneously."

This rally of questions and answers continued. He never left any question take over his confidence. A good farmer is never afraid of the soil he has. He will tilt them, fight them, break them, and make them. This is what his father had taught him.

There will be rains, there will be thunders, but that shouldn't scare the true human. There is always an alternative. This is what his mother taught her.

"Please wait outside. It was good talking to you!" said the figure in center.

He felt confident from within when he heard one of them saying, "quite a presentation. It was good talking to you mister..."

He bowed to them with great respect. He collected his testimonials and certificates that he had carried in inside a file. There were atleast twenty of such certificates. He spoke of his qualifications and the certificates justified his words.

As he left the room, he could hear whispers inside the room.

He waited outside for the results. He had almost given up hope. After a dozen of interviews and the equal number of rejections, he was left with no hope.

It was two in the afternoon. He was getting impatient. He had to catch his bus at three otherwise he would have to wait till seven in the evening until the last bus comes.

He grew impatient when the clock stroke two thirty. He went on to ask when the list would be out. Now? After five minutes? In a moment? When? He was stuck in confusion.

But in all the interviews that he had faced till then, he was most confident in that interview, and he hoped that he would ace it.

It was finally four. His bus was gone. The sky was turning red, giving farewell to sun for the day. Finally at four fifteen the list came out.

Four candidates were selected. He checked the list. Four selections.

First name – not his.

Second name – not his.

Third name – not his.

Fourth name – not his.

Was it his day? Not his!

He looked at his feet. Everywhere they went, they brought misery to him. He pulled his wallet out, he had only fifty rupees. Fourth rupees would be his fare. What would he get for ten rupees?

His quest for success suddenly escalated into a quest for survival.

His hunger was back. He wanted water. He filled his bottle in the premises before leaving and now he had to arrange for his food.

The day was about to end, and he only had had his breakfast as his lone meal. He thought he would return home by afternoon and have his lunch. But it was not possible now.

His bus stop was atleast two kilometers away. He had to walk that distance. By five thirty his tired legs had lifted his sad heart to the bus stand. As soon as he reached there, he saw an old man, almost in his sixties, with grey hairs scattered over his wrinkled skull and sunken eyes opening his shop where he sold sprouts and other things.

"Uncle, please make a plate of ten rupees," he said.

The old man looked up straight at his face and said, "ten? Did you just say ten?"

"Yes," he was desperate. Hunger can make anyone desperate!

"But I don't sell anything below twenty rupees. Atleast twenty. Say if you want, otherwise leave!"

Did he have any other option other than leaving? He left silently and sat on a broken wooden bench as he waited for the bus that would take him to his home.

It was six thirty when someone patted his right shoulder.

He turned back, it was the old man who had sued him earlier. He had a plate of sprouts in his hand.

"Son, forgive me for my misbehavior. Many people in suit and boot come and cheat me. They don't pay me any amount and leave. I thought you were one of those thugs. But You weren't."

His hands wanted to accept the plate, but his conscience deciphered it as alms. But hunger doesn't differentiate between alms and paid food. He took the food and stood up to take his wallet out.

"No son, it's okay! You must be in some deep problem, that's why you asked for a ten rupees plate. Ten rupees won't make me rich."

But he didn't pay any attention to the old man and gave him a ten rupees note, "ten rupees won't make poor either, uncle. Atleast I am not one of those thugs!"

He sat still. Men break too. Men cry too. Opportunities are everywhere, so is failure. If men have more opportunities, doesn't it mean that they must face failure more too? **Boys don't cry**, is it?

At one corner of the stand, he saw four boys standing. They were laughing at each other's joke. One had a bag hung on his shoulder and the other had kept his knees on the seat of his bike. One had an empty paper cup with brown stains on its brim. The other was free from any such connections. He wondered if anyone of them was rejected in their life?

Foolish! Give me a man who isn't broken! A part of men was thrashed so hard as kids that their bonds broke. An other part of men loved so deep that they denied all other bonds and yet they were crushed. Yet there will be another group of men who have been tortured by their wives and children. Where from shall a men supply if he himself has none! Take orders, fulfil them – this is what a family man is. Still some men will be left who have been through all.

Look at the dark spots of men. Look at the wrinkled, tanned foreheads. Look at the old grandfather who still comes to receive his grandchild from school.

Why do grandparents rejoice themselves with their grandchildren? They missed their own sons and daughters grow up. The mother atleast fed then, did the father ever did it? The mother atleast had a chance to pick their child, take into her lap and soothe her crying child. But how often does this happen with the men?

This foolish man doesn't understand that he is not the first neither the last in this line of suffering. He thinks he is grown up, but he isn't.

He wanted strength and he was gifted rejections by the creator.

II
Rangoli

Her sleepy eyes had more dreams than she could actually dream while asleep. All she wanted was some sleep. She wanted to discover her dreamland rather than being a fruit of someone else's dreams.

She curses the apple that fell on Newton. She blesses all the accidents that saved her from such similar tragedies.

Her family was big, but even bigger were the eyes of the members. With a very humongous appetite of not settling for anything other than the best, they had almost fed her soul to tiredness.

"Mother, I cannot!" she said pathetically.

In a very eerie voice, came back a reply, "what? You cannot! What you cannot? And why can't you?"

"I have slept only for twenty hours since last four days!"

"Oh! So, you have started keeping a record of how much time you are sleeping! Have you ever thought of how much time you have read since last four days?"

She had no strength to reply. She didn't want an argument. "How can I mother? How can I read with sleep in my eyes? The letters are unreadable! I don't understand them."

"Are you mad? Look at your cousin, he has been working so hard and he will top in the finals this year! He will then go to some good college after twelfth!"

She replied, "am I not in eleventh standard now mother?"

"You have only a year left, and you think it's too much?" asked her mother.

Breaking this chat between the mother-daughter, entered the solid rock. "What are you talking about?" asked his father from behind.

She went straight to her father, and hugged her tight, "father, I can't. I just can't take any more! I am tired. Please relieve me!"

Her father patted her back and warmly kept his hands on her shoulder. He wiped his sleepy eyes and tired face! He grabbed a bottle of water from the corner and opened the cap for her.

"Here, have some water. You will feel better!" he said.

It was almost seven in the evening. Her mother was busy cooking food for the family; for it was her turn to make the food that day.

Their house had a strange rotation policy. The three daughters-in-law cooked for two days each. Six days were managed in such way and Sunday was their day of unity.

"Where is the chili powder?" would scream the first.

The second would reply, "what chili powder? Don't you remember last time you had used it up all?"

"Ah! Don't forget that my husband too earns for this family. He doesn't put his money into some rathole. He had got the chili powder from market few days back only and you say you cannot find it? There must be a packetful of it!" would join the third.

Is there a house where no such lovely bombings happen?

"Father, I need some time to rest now. You see, it's only the month of July and I have completed ninety percent of the eleventh syllabus. There are things that are not even taught to me in tuitions. And in school, they are just in second chapter. I am well ahead of time!" she pleaded.

"For how much time is she here?" her mother was asked.

She replied, "for almost five minutes!"

He turned towards her, "had you not wasted this much time pleading here, you could have completed another sum in mathematics or might have remembered another theorem from physics. Look *beta*, I don't want you to be behind that crooked nephew of mine."

"I know father, you have told this atleast a thousand of times."

Her mother replied, "so let him say a lakh times more until you understand this!"

She had no answer on her side. What could have she said? She was tried, wasn't she? She told her problem, didn't she? She wasn't heard, was she? She was just a junior in among a bunch of seniors competing for some place.

Who doesn't want a break?

"Mother, my friends are going out for a film. It's a good film, can I join them please?" she asked few days later. Somewhere deep in her, she knew what was coming.

"Yes, why not!" her mother replied.

A bright smile spread across her lips. "Seriously mother!"

"Yes, I am serious."

"Thank you so much mother. Thank you so much. I was so bored with this life." She ran and hugged her mother.

Her mother hugged her back tightly. She kept her palms on her head and ran them through her long, black hair. "Yes, you have my permission to go, but only after you complete your finals."

When to leave, where to leave and where and when not to leave, everything was decided for her. Decisions are strange things, aren't they?

She freed herself from the clutch and looked at her. Like a stone rolling down a cliff complains of being hurt from other spiky stones; like a falling leaf complains about a newborn leaf that forced her away from the tree; like a shooting star complaining the air about the resistance; her eyes too had complains.

She left heartbroken.

Drop after drop, tears rolled down her cheeks and fell on her books. Her visibility was gone. Her eyes were lost behind the cloud of tears like sun lost behind the cloud of water.

She wanted to throw her books away, burn her notes and break her pens. She wanted to splatter the ink all around her.

She questioned her birth. "Was I born at the wrong time? Was I born at the wrong place? What is wrong with me? Was it my mistake that I became someone's cousin? Was it my fault that I became a girl? Was it all my fault at all?"

Can't she take steps backwards?

She wanted strength and she was gifted chains by the creator.

III

Aisha

A free cockroach is free till he finds a healthy litter. Its pity, she isn't a roach.

"To love and be loved is the best feeling ever," she exclaimed!

"Did anyone propose you?" someone among her friends asked her.

"What? Why would anyone propose me?" she replied.

They perhaps thought a new love story was brewing somewhere. Anything new is a new issue of discussion. Beauty comes and goes, but not the discussion about it!

"Life is always in sync with lies," he whispered into her ears.

She was lost in his arms with butterflies in her stomach! It was dark and like any star shining in dark, they looked like a couple of fireflies from a great distant.

"What now?" he asked. He must be expecting something, isn't it? A cool evening, with no one around to disturb, what can be done in the silence and loneliness? A mug or coffee or a cup of coffee would have been a great idea, isn't it?

But alas they thought hugging was a better idea.

"Your arms are so strong!" she said.

He hugged her tighter, "you are as tinder as a flower!"

She released herself from the clasp of his hands, "what? I am tender! You think I am tender?"

He was stunned. Infact I too was. "What else you are? Your skin is so soft, I think I will break it if I touch you hard. I find you so fragile, I fear I will break you if I lift you from your waist! You are lovely, but tender."

Indeed, lies are always in sync with life. Had there been no sync she would not have hugged her back then.

Sitting in the backyard of her house, on the green lushy grass in the spring evening, they were ready to lose each into the other. It was their night!

"You are so beautiful," he said.

She said, "you are equally handsome!"

I wonder, how could they decide who was beautiful and who was handsome in that darkness? Did they see each other's inner beauty?

"Till when things will carry on?" she asked.

"Till then when things don't run out of control!" he replied.

Things between them were as safe as a safe kept in a vault. No one knew and they met every day. She lived alone in the house and that gave him the freedom that he wanted.

It was evening, morning, noon and afternoon, there was no fixed time when he would drop by. Indeed, he would drop by to drop in.

One such day, they had a strong discussion. He claimed, "one should never believe a snake, river, fire and a woman!"

She took on her aggressive stance. "Why? Why do you think so?"

"First of all, snake! I personally won't believe a snake. A creature who slithers into dry leaves. I hate everyone and every creature who camouflages! And snake mastering this technique must never be believed. Who knows when that wild creature will twist to insert its dirty venomous fangs?"

"Okay, next," she said.

"A river also must never be believed. No one can ever say when a river will overflow or take a turn. No one knows when it will run dry or the exact depth. It takes everything with it. It can never be believed."

"Very banal! Okay next!"

"Fire is also dangerous. A little spark can ignite a fire that can consume a whole locality within no moment! How can I ever believe fire!"

"I won't appreciate it, but okay. I want to know why women? Do we slither? Do we take everything? Do we consume localities in a span of moment?"

He replied, "no things are not like that. Only slithering doesn't make anything awkward."

I think he wanted to point out the slithering of faces beneath makeups and powder for a perfect camouflage!

He continued, "nor does only overflowing or drying up makes something unreliable!"

He must be trying to say about emotions which have no steady flow!

He further said, "a spark can be made from anywhere. Fire doesn't discriminate between what it can burn!"

He perhaps succeeded in saying his heart out this time.

"Then why are we women included in this list of fatality?" she questioned.

"Well, you see this saying is quite old and back then women didn't step out to face the world, so they had the least idea of how the world ran! So, taking any suggestion from them would be fatal. It is something like asking a flute player how to play chess!" he replied. He thought he had escaped.

"Are we fools now too?" she asked.

"Of course not! You are reliable. I rely on you, don't I? There must have been women who would have cheated on men and that found its outlet in that quote!" He somehow could suppress the fire that might have lit then instantly.

Still a flame had escaped before the damage control, "do only women cheat? Are all men really loyal?"

Fire, such a strange thing, it burns anything that comes in its way. The vermillion flames are eternally hungry. The fire in him grew so much a few days later that he too lost something to the flames.

As usual, she was on her way to her workplace.

"Hi!" she met Neha on the way, one of her colleagues.

"Hey!" wished her back.

They went on, climbed the stairs as usual, discussing about breakfast.

"Hey, did you hear about the sale?" Neeti joined them.

And as if this was the missing spark.

"What? Where?" she jumped in straight.

Neeti explained some shop in some dense corner of their city.

"What? Is there a shop there?" asked Neha.

Neeti confirmed it. "They have some very good products. My boyfriend has gifted me a vanity bag and it is so good. It was cheap but it gives the vibe of something exclusive."

Vanity! Indeed Vanity.

But she had something more to confirm. She texted her lover, "are you showing up tonight?"

After almost five minutes came the reply, "don't know. Have any plans?"

"No, I have no such plans!"

She replied, "okay!"

Things went on as it were to happen. It was the break time and she called him.

"Hey!"

He responded back, "Hi!"

In the most childish manner, she said, "well... I was planning to go some shopping tonight!"

"With me?"

"Neha and Neeti will join me," she said.

As if he was rejuvenated, "oh! Have a great evening. I will wrap up some pending work then and see you tomorrow!"

"Sure!" she replied.

"See you soon! Take care!"

A month passed. When it doesn't rain for a long time, prepare the best of your boats!

On a usual day, she reached her office. "Hey Neeti!" Her greetings had a different tone.

"Hi! You chirp like a sparrow, what has happened?" she winked.

"Nothing like that. One of my closest friends is getting engaged tonight. Just excited for the event."

"Oh wow! Congratulate her from my side. Many many happy wishes from my side."

They walked into their cubicle. "Why don't you join me?"

"Me! Oh no... I am unknown to her. It will be rude if I join uninvited." She pounced replied.

"There is nothing rude in that. I assure you. You won't find yourself cornered!"

She knew she would be surrounded by her with girls like her – young and beautiful. But she was in no mood to join. What followed was nothing but arrows of please, yes, and no!

Curiosity is a very stupid thing. When you hear a lot about something, your eyes get jealous of your ears. They too want their piece of cake.

"No Neeti, don't force me. I won't be comfortable there. But just show me their pics, a couple pic maybe."

"Sure, why not!" She put her hand into her bag and pulled her phone out.

In a whip like spin, she moved her phone. Like a customer who examines a gold chain after the goldsmith passes on her hand, she looked at the corners searching for dust. She wiped the phone her phone on her denim.

She pressed the lock key. She smiled looking at the front camera, hoping the facecam to work and unlock handsfree. One try... Two tries... Three tries... and she exceeded her limit.

"Crap!"

She swiped her lock screen up. Buzz... Buzz... Buzz... Buzz... She pressed her pin and unlocked her phone. She swiped the home screen up and opened her gallery.

"Here!" she passed on her phone to her.

The smile changed into a frown and the expecting eyes stuck to the phone.

"Is he your friend's..."

Before he could complete herself, she jumped in, "yes, don't they look cute together?"

"Oh yes, they do!" she wanted to smile, but her lips refused. She wanted to cry, but her eyes refused. She wanted to scream, but her voice refused. She was the refused!

She quietly passed her her phone and got back to her desk. With great ease she controlled her emotions.

In the break she called her lover.

"Hello!" never in her life had she said hello.

"Hey!" he was happy.

She asked her, "why don't you come over tonight? Let's dine together. It's been some time since we have spent some time together."

"Tonight?" his voice had refusal hidden.

"Yes... Are you busy tonight?"

"Well... kind of. I have some work to finish!" he replied.

"Okay then! Better someday other."

He confirmed, "yes!" She hung the call.

She texted him, "congratulations for your new beginning! It will be a new life for you and for her too. As I withdraw into my life of solace and silence do not try to invade it. If ever you try to contact me, I will be at my worst. It was my misfortune I met you, you were fortunate enough that I met you. I feel how it feels it be used and you must be feeling great after using. I have an option to attend your ceremony, but tonight I ceremonially shall coffin my emotions. So, I will be busy! You should have invited me; an invitation wouldn't have hurt much than this hiding. Don't ever try to make any contact with me, you cheat!"

She was left alone now. She changed her city and now she has nothing left in her. Life goes on just like sun rising and sun setting.

She wanted strength and she was gifted betrayal by the creator.

IV
Smita

Where from do ambitions come? Do ambitions come coupled with freedom? Isn't freedom just a sweet myth?

"I take with me pain; I take with me memories and I don't know what else can I carry in this little suitcase of mine?" she asked herself.

She looked outside, through her windows. The sky was clear, it was cold. A shiver ran through her body. Her spines shuddered.

"Nothing stops in this world. Nothing goes a waste except for your blood that you shed every month," his boyfriend was screaming at her.

She didn't say anything. She was silent. A cat plays with a rat before eating it; she felt like that helpless rat who could do nothing and run stretches between the two furry paws. In no time the rat would be a dead piece of meat!

She cried in deep silence. She thought of leaving everything and run away to some far place, like sun hiding beneath the horizon after the night came.

Humen are very crazy creatures. They seek happiness, like any other creatures, but they take happiness as an obsession.

"Too much of faith is destructive!" her best friend had once warned her.

She had rendered herself to him with such an intensity that she had no time to think twice before she left her home.

"The step you are taking today is the step for which I kick you out of my house," her father's words were echoing in her ears.

She was built different like all girls are made equally distinctive from each other. No two poisons are same!

"See Vikrant, I am leaving everything for you, please do not leave me." A man when is in desperate need of something will commit about anything and everything. And he committed too.

She thought with this liberation she would become independent. Her ambition of becoming independent was denser than her conscience. She forgot that life needs verification. Everything must be verified. Did he ever verify Vikrant before she offered herself to him?

But what about the commitment that was born with him? His family!

They had a bitter fight. Vikrant's family wanted him to get rid of her and get back home. They had selected a girl of their choice. He was confused, but when you have to choose between two things – one with whom you have spent much longer time than the other, you generally tend to pick the most known thing. It gives the sense of security.

It was sure that she would be left alone.

What does it take to merely exist? Money? She had enough of it in her account. She had more than she could spend. That night she begged him, held him by his legs and he still left.

It was better for her to vacant that room too! What would she do in a room that was too small to hold her tears. She had decided to change her address and move into some other town.

The whole night she sat next to the window, lighting cigarettes after cigarettes. She was lost.

"This is so tasty," her father enjoyed the meal that she had made.

Her mother said, "it's too good for someone cooking for the first time."

She was creative. First the oil, then onions, then masalas and then the fresh chicken. As if she were the chicken now – helpless and squeaking for help.

Like a butcher goes and picks a chicken randomly to shred the feathers and cut the flesh and bones into pieces, he too had broken her into pieces.

She had cooked the same recipe for Vikrant when they first decided to move in. Wasn't he happy that day? Yes, he was. He praised her high for her cooking skills. Where have the praise gone now? Where did she lose everything?

"Oh, a shooting star!" she exclaimed. She threw the half burnt white stick out though the window and closed his eyes.

She did nothing but waited, waited for the day to come. She wanted to leave everything and retire silently.

"Hey!" it was Vikrant. It was seven in the morning.

"Hi!" was he coming back? Did he too feel uneasy the same way she felt? In a flash she lost all the pain of last night.

After a pause, "what are you doing?"

"I am doing nothing. What happened?" she replied as soon as he asked without a second spent on thinking.

The pollen that gives life, too gives allergy! "You were packing your bags! Are you done with it?" he asked.

She was sure that he would again scold and ask her to put her things back. "Yes, almost!"

With a voice colder than the previous night he said, "actually... I was thinking to move in into that house with Sunayana!"

A girl? Who is she? "Sunayana? Who is she?"

As if she had rehearsed what he would say when confronted with the question, he said, "my family has chosen her, we will be getting engaged soon. But before any such commitment I thought it was better on our parts that we get to know each other better!"

She would have survived if she were coffined alive, but it was not her body that was coffined with the answer, it was her soul.

"What? Commitment!" he had crossed his limit.

She continued, "you speak of commitment? You drove me out of my house, now you say that you are committed to her? Wasn't I committed to you? Do not think that I have forgotten things. It's been five years that I have been with you. At what point, just for god's sake, just give me a point when I have disappointed you. Yes, I bleed, yes, I do. What is the problem in that? I am not an old woman, I still young. Don't young ladies bleed? Go ask your mother. You say of family. Whose family teaches their son to get connected to a girl and then just leave? You think it was a game. You think it, don't you? Well yes, it was just a love game. I should have understood your intensions for love was never in your dictionary. You proposed me for the sake of a challenge that your friends had given. You texted me for the sake of that damn challenge. I was a fool, yes, I was a fool that I believed your emotions to be true. Do not forget this, that my submission to you was a game of mine. Throughout these years, I have tolerated you, and sorry for the displeasure that I caused you last night. Your masculinity was at its peak and so was my femininity."

Before hanging up the call, he said, "vacant the room as quick as possible."

Just the room, her life too had an irreplaceable vacancy!

She wanted strength and she was gifted loneliness by the creator.

V
The Moving Bus

The bus moved on and on. Flashes of streetlight at times luminated her face. But that light made him look spooky.

A bus stop came. The bus stopped heavily leaving a cloud of dust behind.

Six feet climbed in. Three ladies after a busy day got on the bus. Who were they?

One of them was gifted chains, the second was gifted betrayal and the third was gifted loneliness. They never knew they were so similar to each other and yet they were different. They were so close to each other and yet they were far from each other.

Each of them observed the boy sitting on the backseat with flashes on his rusty face. They felt uncomfortable. They outnumbered him, yet they felt keenly insecure.

"Hey!" Rangoli looked through the top of her glasses and wished the other two girls.

The other two wished her back, "do you look at that guy?" asked Smita.

"Yes, I too was about to say that too, he looks like a culprit," said Aisha.

They took seat next to each other. "He looks so professional, look at that shirt and blazer," said Smita.

"Oh yes," they took turns to turn back as they turned their head little at one time to scan the poor boy.

"I don't know why I am getting sadistic vibes from him," said Rangoli.

"As if he were to commit some crime and jump out of the bus." The trio laughed after Aisha said that.

"It was a busy day at the office. The boss screamed so loud. I thought of murdering that fellow right there," said Smita.

Rangoli laughed. "I am quite junior to you!"

"How does that even matter? Senior or junior, you are one among us and like us," said Smita.

"This is my second year of medical coaching here," replied Rangoli.

"Where are you going so late then?" asked Smita.

"I am returning to my hostel. I had a test today and missed the afternoon bus," she replied.

Aisha said, "I at least had an average day then. I was out with my friends for a movie."

"You go for movies?" asked Rangoli.

"Yes, all go! What's new in that?" added Smita.

"You guys are lucky. That's what I think life will be when I will grow up!" said Rangoli.

"Stressed for exams?" asked Aisha. Rangoli agreeingly nodded her head.

"Who isnt? I am still not secured. I have the job today, who knows when I will be relived from my post?" joked Aisha.

"That's not the only thing. Sometimes you also need to keep a check on what you earn and how much you spend? I am new to this place, and I am discovering this place with a newly made friend," said Smita.

Floodgates were about to be opened. No matter how hard he tried to restrain himself, he couldn't. He couldn't hit at the interviewers. The wild horse wanted to gallop. As the night came upon, he could gather no more courage. He wanted a vent out, and he jumped in.

Why? I don't know. This is only known to him.

"Yes, you all are right!" a masculine voice added from behind. He continued, "I beg your pardon for interrupting and invading your privacy. But couldn't stop myself from jumping in."

"Don't you have any manners?" questioned Smita.

"Yes, I do have them. For me no one is culprit no matter what dress he or she wears. Dress can be changed. They are just like present address, today here tomorrow someplace else!"

"That still doesn't validate your interference in our conversation." Said Aisha.

"Need not worry little girl, the stress that you feel now, will be a boon in near future. The stress that you feel today, will be like nothing that will face tomorrow."

"Thanks for the free advice but she doesn't need it actually," defended Aisha.

"A good ship can be built at the shore, but not a good sailor!" he replied. "You will have to fight the towering waves and tear through them. If you cannot, I won't use sweet lies to coax you, but you will fail."

Things started getting hot from this point. He perhaps couldn't tolerate him being trolled for nothing.

"That's the problem with you boys, you feel that girls are your toys. Any toy you see, you want to earn them!" said Aisha.

"No, I do not believe in that," he replied gently.

"Then what do you believe in?" asked Smita,

"It doesn't matter what I believe in. It matters what you believe in."

Rangoli who was silent for a while just couldn't hold back her. "Stop with all your nonsense. Please, do not argue. I already have lots of problems. It's not just how my day went on! But the day that is yet to come. As a stranger, please maintain the least of ethics, please don't break the thumb rule of strangers being not so rude to other travelling fellows."

"I had never breached anyone's privacy. I am just here for my defense," he replied.

"Mr. whosoever you are, you have taken enough of your side. I think it's enough for us today and you may leave now,' said Smita.

"Little girl, I don't find your parents wrong when they force you to read and write. They are trying for your better tomorrow."

Rangoli roared this time, "seriously? For last four years, I haven't slept peacefully! For last four years I am looking for recreation, but that I don't have."

"Oh!"

"What? Oh? It is just for another male like you that I am facing this torture!" Rangoli said.

"Who is that another male like me?" he asked.

She let out a breath of fire. "My cousin. He cracked NEET in his second attempt and is just a year senior to me."

"So you dedicate your suffering to males and men!" he asked.

"Hell yes! Don't you understand? You are the problem that we don't want. Without you we will have no problems!"

He smiled. He nodded his head. "Oh yes! We are the problem. We are definitely the problem. But have you ever tried to escape for it?"

"Escape? This world is yours; you made the laws. Infact, you are the laws!" Rangoli was unstoppable.

It seemed as if some latent force drove them native!

He laughed. "And you think we reached to this point all by ourselves. Was it so easy to escape the grip that you had over family? Was it that easy to crush you females ages and ages back? Then sadly, I must say that you were just too crippled to overpower us. No cripple has the right to rule. This is what the nature wants. If all survive, then nothing will survive. And look back at your history miss, you were a powerful half of an even more powerful species. We are not heard about! Our physical strength restricts us from crying and sadly you find a crying boy cute, and we find a crying girl sad."

"Don't pull nature into this thing. You men don't understand nature. Had you understood what nature is, you wouldn't have blamed us. Nature is ever-progressive. Anything that nature gave us, must be for a reason!" Smita jumped in.

"Oh! Yes, nature made us different. But nature must have had a reason. But what has nature given us? The title of thugs, the tag of a traitor? The way you are tied to chains, we too are!"

"You say it's our fault?" asked Aisha.

"No! it's not your fault. I don't know whose. Look around you, how many sad faces you see? We just are in a race for the sake of running. We don't know what the bounty is! I don't know why you are often physically tortured; I don't know why we cry in silence. I don't know why you are cheated, and also, I don't know why we are cheated for? Look at the patency of this life. You do the same as we, and yet we go unnoticed. Respect for the silkworm that died unremarked!"

Smita said, "for you we women are just things of beauty!"

"A woman is not just an object of beauty!"

"Then why do you guys in hunt for looking another girl? Is it that easy?" asked Smita.

"But won't I look at what I want! Why will I look at something that I don't want? You have beauty in you, so you don't want to look for that in your friend. But the thing that I don't have in me, I will go hunting it! Won't I?" He was growing impatient from within.

His frustration wanted him to do something violent and get rid of the anarchial creatures seated right before him. But culture held his hand and pulled him back.

The girls too did want to react, but, their culture held their hand and pulled them back!

They all were free, yet they weren't.

"It's you men who have shut down the doors at our face of opportunity. You are nothing more than opportunists."

The bus stopped with a jerk and his destination was there.

"This reminds me of a funny incident. The culprit whom you thought to commit grave crimes went for an interview today and four selections were made after the interview. Sarcastically, all the four candidates were females. Yes, I am taking things for granted and I feel you must have felt the same. And I respect you for that, you bore it all. Yes, we made rules, yes, we set them, but we also took ourselves into that. Don't you think it will actually be funny if a fully grown man comes out wearing a saree. If we set the standard of saree for you, we also set the standard of not wearing a saree."

No one spoke but him. "If you think we are shutting the door for you, yes, we might have done it in the past. But right now, in the present its you who are shutting the doors for us. Tit for tat! And I am okay with that. Things must be repaid. And still if you think that you are weak, you are poor, you are unmarvelous, then with all due respect you are wrong. Come out of this bubble and I must mention this that it was my thirteenth interview. Only one such interview was there when only one male candidate was selected! I feel sad for that guy, he must be feeling the same awkwardness as a new bride in her in-laws faces among the menfolk. Taking orders must have been a hard task for you all, but it is hard for us too. We just don't say it. We have chocked our emotions!"

He went back to his seat, collected his papers and file. With slow and disbalanced steps he moved towards the door. "Good luck!"

They all wanted strength and they were gifted life by...

About Cover Page

Emotions are basic to humans, and particularly to men. We do not see them expessing themselves.

Life and pain go hand in hand and can never be separated from each other. That is what this cover page attempts to do.

Some may find the cover funny, and I have no problem with that. Spreading smiles is a virtue!

End Note

As mentioned earlier, I have reserved certain part for future works. Consciously, I will not let anything go away without writing them in my works.

I offer my sincerest gratitude to the womenfolk who have for years now been indoor beasts of burden. I extend my smpathies and wishes to the menfolk who have for years now been outdoor beasts of burden.

Men have always been central to any society. They are documented at almost every step. We have datas for what male workforce we have, but somewehere we have lacked in providing females the same documentation. The case is not exclusive to workforce, rather it extends to almost every sphere of the society.

If anywhere I have hurt any sentiments, I apologize unconditionally.

Get In Touch

Facebook - Raudra Series
Instagram - raudra.series
E-Mail - raudra.series@gmail.com